KT-498-321

CHARLES DARWIN'S

AROUND-THE-WORLD ADVENTURE

JENNIFER THERMES

ABRAMS BOOKS FOR YOUNG READERS • NEW YORK

CHARLES ROBERT DARWIN would have rather been outside searching for bugs, beetles, worms, butterflies, birds, rocks, and bones than sitting in a classroom. His teachers didn't think he was very smart. But Charles spent hours sorting through the treasures he found.

Charles loved collecting.

Once, when his hands were full with two beetles, he plopped a third one into his mouth to bring it home. It squirted something bitter and he had to spit it out. Charles was sad to lose that beetle.

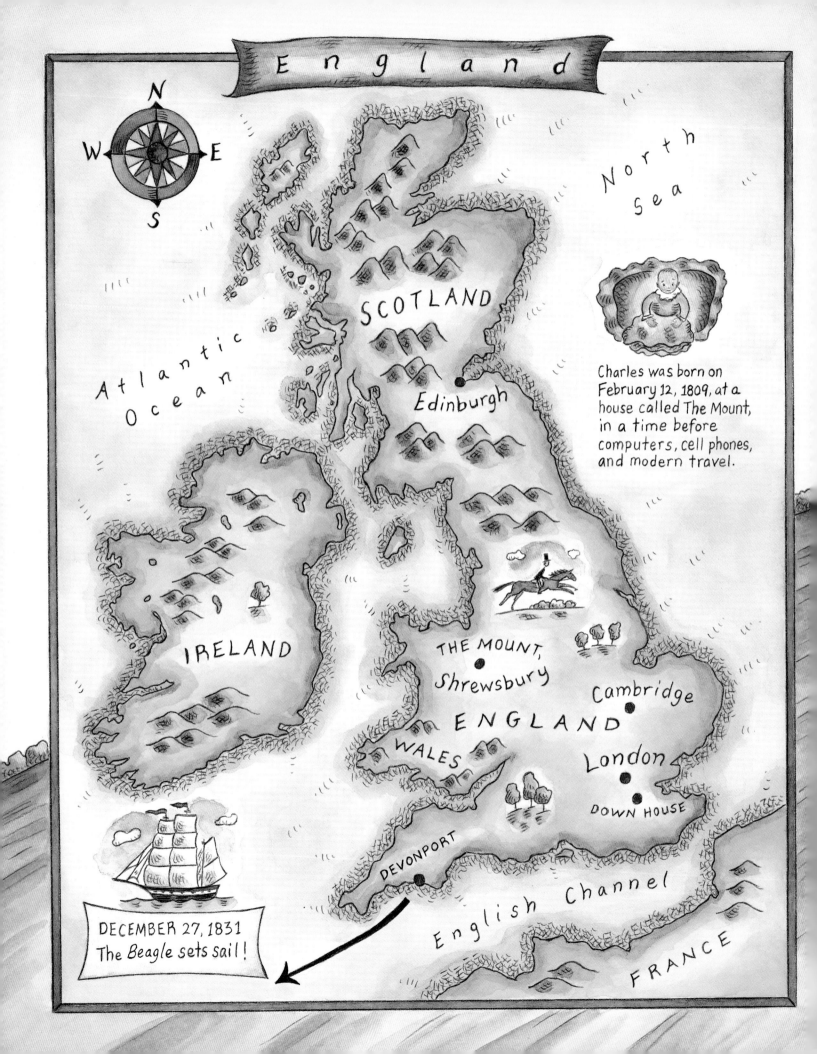

England

SCOTLAND

Edinburgh

North Sea

Atlantic Ocean

Charles was born on February 12, 1809, at a house called The Mount, in a time before computers, cell phones, and modern travel.

IRELAND

THE MOUNT, Shrewsbury

Cambridge

ENGLAND

WALES

London

DOWN HOUSE

DEVONPORT

English Channel

FRANCE

DECEMBER 27, 1831
The *Beagle* sets sail!

Charles tried to be a doctor like his father, but the sight of blood made him queasy. So he studied to become a clergyman. While attending Cambridge University, he took long walks with his professors, exploring the countryside. It was his favorite part of school.

After graduation, Charles's professor of botany wrote a letter recommending him to be the naturalist aboard the HMS *Beagle*. The ship's mission was to take map measurements of South America. Charles would be able to explore new places all around the world! He was thrilled.

His father thought it was a "wild scheme," but he finally let Charles go.

The *Beagle* set sail heading west around the globe. She was only ninety feet long and packed tight with sailors and supplies. A man named Robert FitzRoy was her captain. Charles was very seasick, but the excitement of seeing palm trees and an island made by a volcano soon made him forget the ocean swells.

On a tiny group of rocks in the middle of the sea, he decided he would write about all he saw on his journey.

ENGLAND

EUROPE

Devonport

Atlantic Ocean

Tenerife

Cape Verde Islands

AFRICA

St. Paul Rock

THE EQUATOR

SOUTH AMERICA

Bahia, BRAZIL

In the rain forest, the ground soaked up the downpour while the plants grew green and lush. Charles was surrounded by the buzz of millions of insects, yet the jungle wrapped him in velvet silence.

The landscape was so different from anything Charles had known in England. He was giddy.

East Coast ~ South America

N W E S

Brazilian Wandering Spider

12-Foot-Tall Anthill

Bahia

Agouti

B R A Z I L

Hyla Frog

Burrowing Owl

Blue Morpho Butterfly

Botafogo

Rio de Janeiro

Santa Fe

URUGUAY

A R G E N T I N A

PAMPAS

Buenos Aires

Montevideo

RÍO DE LA PLATA

Bahía Blanca

Punta Alta

Stick insects disguise themselves from predators for protection. Charles saw how creatures change shape and color in order to survive.

He collected butterflies, beetles,
spiders, and lizards to send back home.
At the end of every day, he wrote in
his journal. He made big observations
about the tiniest of creatures.

Charles was happy to stay on land and explore while the *Beagle* sailed up and down the coast. The land *didn't* churn his stomach and make his head spin! He galloped with gauchos across the dry plains of the pampas and camped at night with his saddle for a pillow.

Charles found eight kinds of mice and giant fossil teeth. He saw a
rare bird called a rhea that used its wings to steer as it ran, but could not
fly. He discovered that some creatures were good for eating. Roasted
armadillo made a tasty breakfast.

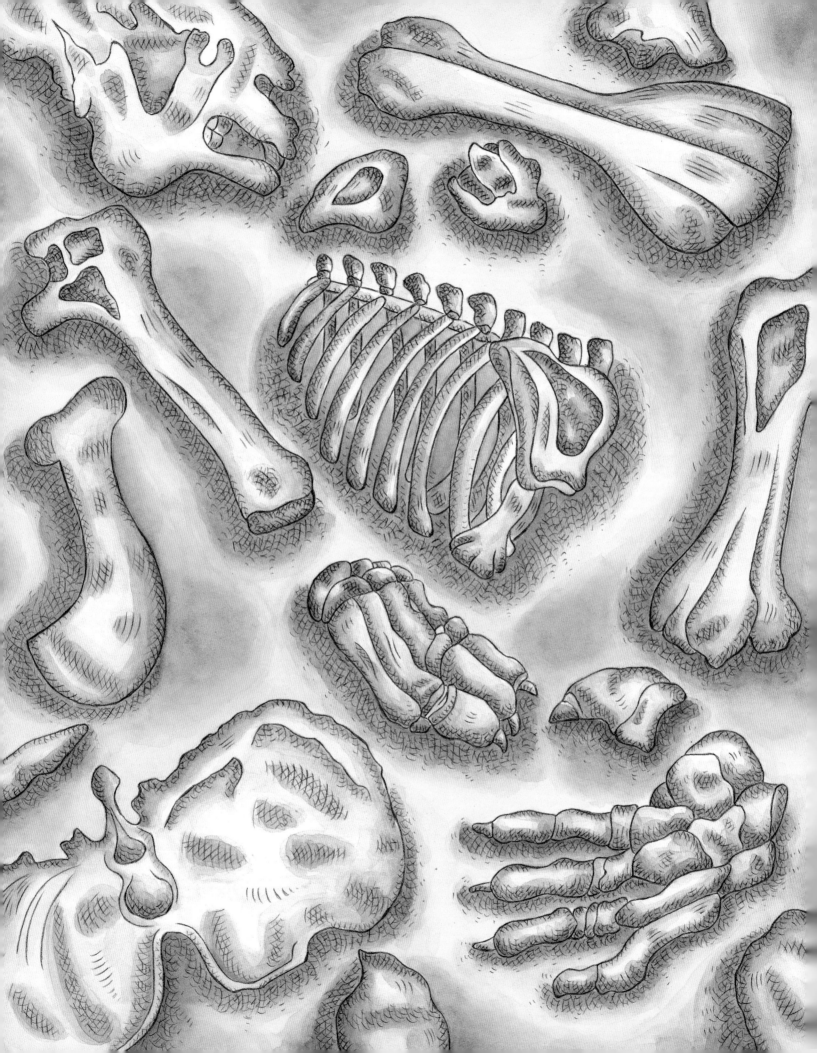

Charles dug up bones of ancient sloth-like creatures, including a giant Megatherium, buried on the beach. How many of these huge creatures once roamed the earth? Why had they disappeared?

He studied the rocks and tried to figure out how steep cliffs and flat plains were formed. Was it possible that the shape of the land affected the animals' survival?

Jackass Penguins

Seals

Strait of Magellan

Cape Horn

N
W E
S

Egret

Falkland Islands

Tierra del Fuego

Beagle Channel

The *Beagle* sailed farther south through rough seas, as wind and rain whipped the sturdy ship.

Once, Charles, Captain FitzRoy, and a few sailors were exploring the shoreline in small boats, one hundred miles from the *Beagle*. Suddenly, a huge chunk of ice crashed from a glacier into the sea. The wave it made almost destroyed their vessels. The men were lucky. It would have been nearly impossible to survive in the cold, desolate land, with no way to call for help.

The weather was so bad it took almost a month to try to sail around Cape Horn. They finally had to turn back and cross through the Strait of Magellan.

Under the frigid waters of Tierra del Fuego, forests of seaweed waved back and forth, teeming with life. The kelp was food for fish and crabs and microscopic creatures, which in turn fed birds and otters and seals.

The bigger animals couldn't survive without eating the smaller ones. Charles saw how their lives were all connected.

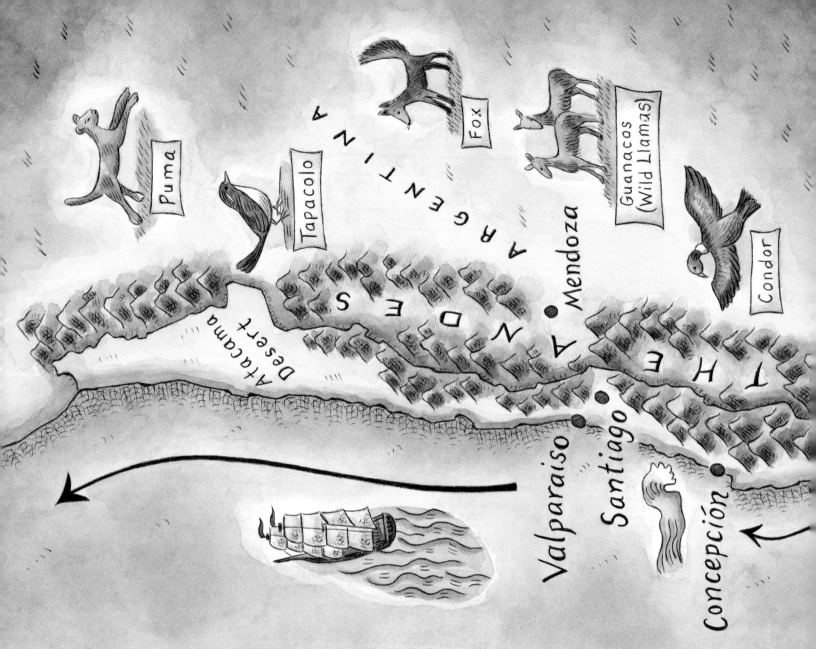

The *Beagle* zigzagged up and down the long coast of Chile, while Charles
took trips through the countryside, meeting the ship along the way.

A chain of mountains towered over the land. How had they become so huge?

One night—*BOOM!*—a volcano exploded, like fireworks in the sky. A few
weeks later the ground groaned and shifted. The earth rumbled far within, and
a massive quake shook the land. Charles was two hundred miles away from
the center of the earthquake, but he wrote in his journal that it felt like he was
standing on thin ice.

Far out at sea, a giant wave formed from the motion of the earth and rolled toward shore. It swallowed villages and swept them away.

When Charles saw the destruction, he was shocked. But he noticed that the earth was a few feet higher than it had been before. Could the volcano and the earthquake and the changes to the land be related?

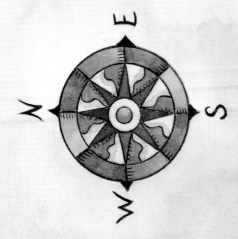

He found his answer up, up, up—in the rose-colored
shadows and snowy peaks of the Andes Mountains.

Seashells! Fossilized seashells were embedded in the rocks, thousands of feet above the ocean!

Charles was sure that the Andes must have been under water a long, long time ago, and that the earth was always shifting from deep inside— sometimes slowly, sometimes suddenly. With enough time, these movements could make mountains higher than clouds in the sky.

He was so excited by his discovery that he forgot how hard it was to breathe in the thin mountain air.

After almost four years of exploring, it was time to start the long voyage home. But first, the *Beagle* would stop at an archipelago more than five hundred miles off the coast of South America, called . . .

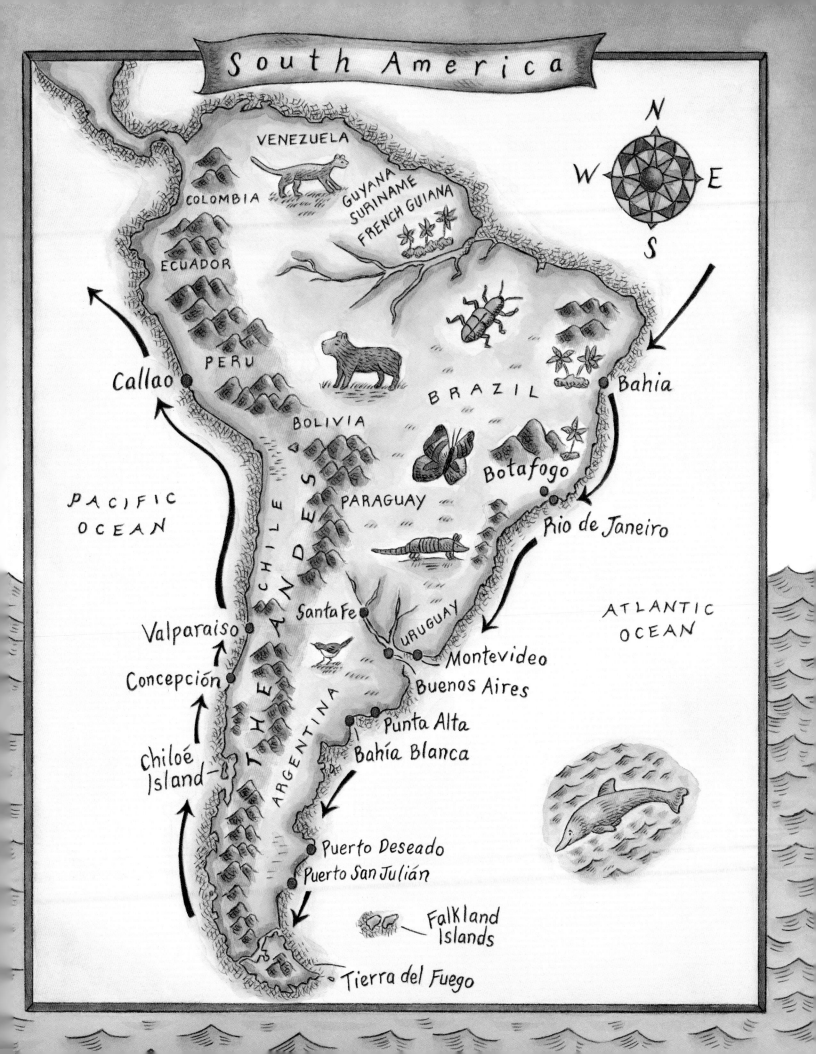

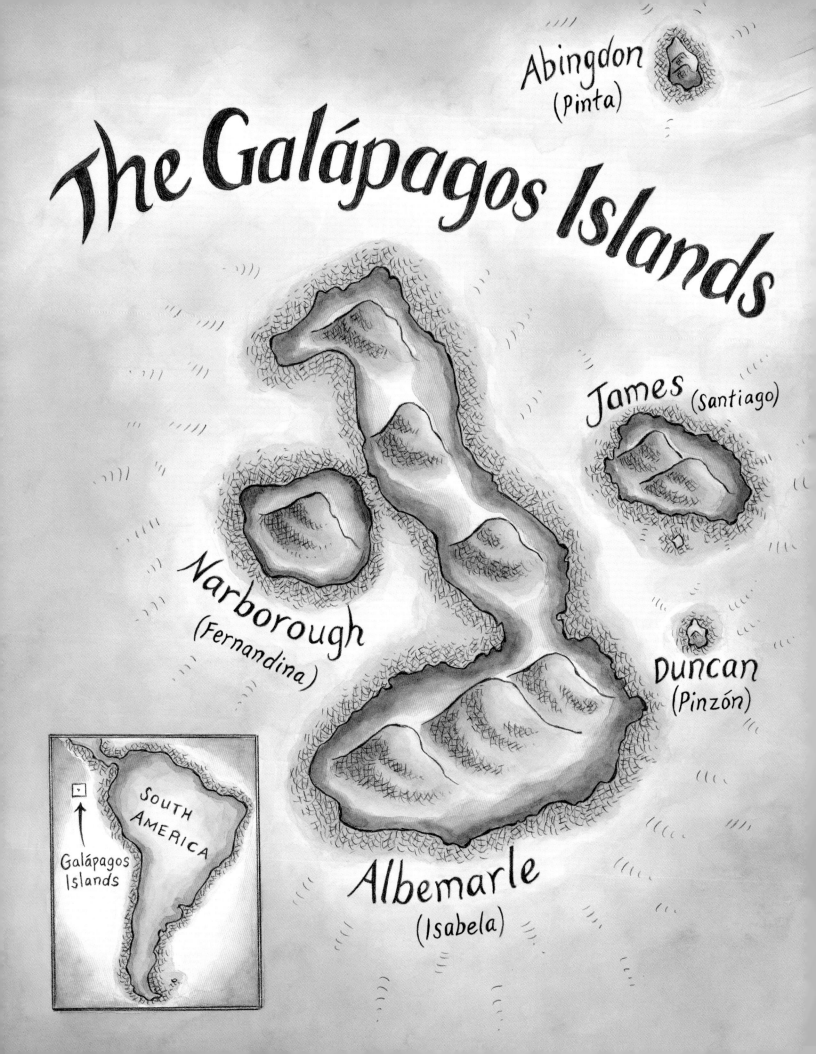

Bindloe
(Marchena)

Tower

. . . the Galápagos Islands. Charles had never
seen anything like them.

Indefatigable
(Santa Cruz)

Barrington
(Santa Fe)

Chatham
(San Cristóbal)

Charles
(Floreana)

Hood (Española)

Flightless
Cormorant

Player Scorpion Fish

Blue-Footed Booby

Magnificent
Frigate Bird

Galápagos Hawk

The islands were made of black
volcanic rock. Charles was amazed
at the creatures in this isolated
place, surrounded by the sea. They
were not afraid of humans! It was
magical.

There were four-foot-long
lizards that lived on the beach but
hated water. And there were two-
hundred-pound tortoises, big
enough for Charles to try to ride.

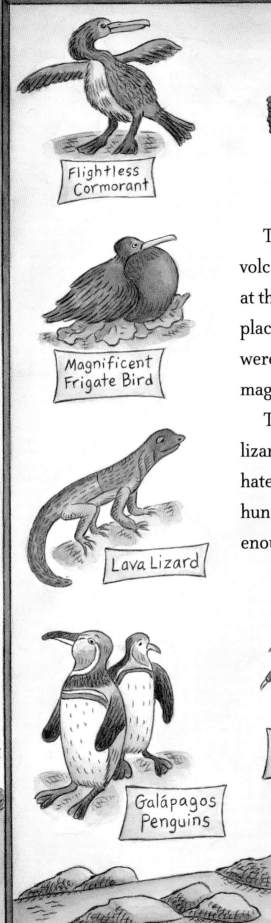

Lava Lizard

Galápagos
Fur Seal

Sally Lightfoot
Crab

Galápagos
Penguins

Galápagos Land Iguana

Charles counted many kinds of finches across the islands.
They were related to one another, yet birds from different islands
had different-shaped beaks. He wondered why.

Years later, Charles learned that some finches had small
beaks because they ate tiny seeds, and some had big beaks strong
enough to crack hard seeds. Their beaks had changed over time
depending on what food they ate. The birds had adapted to where
they lived.

The *Beagle* spent one month wandering around the Galápagos, then headed west again.

The ship was stocked full with barrels of water and food—including tortoises for eating. Crates full of rocks, shells, insects, birds, and bones packed every corner. Sometimes the sailors were annoyed because Charles's treasures cluttered the deck. But after years of traveling together, they admired how hard he worked.

As the *Beagle* blew across the sea, Charles spent hours in his cramped cabin organizing his notes and specimens and writing in his journal. He was beginning to have new ideas about how the earth was formed and how animals evolved in order to survive. All that he had seen so far was making sense.

Charles now knew for sure that he would be a scientist when he returned to England. The natural world would be his life's work.

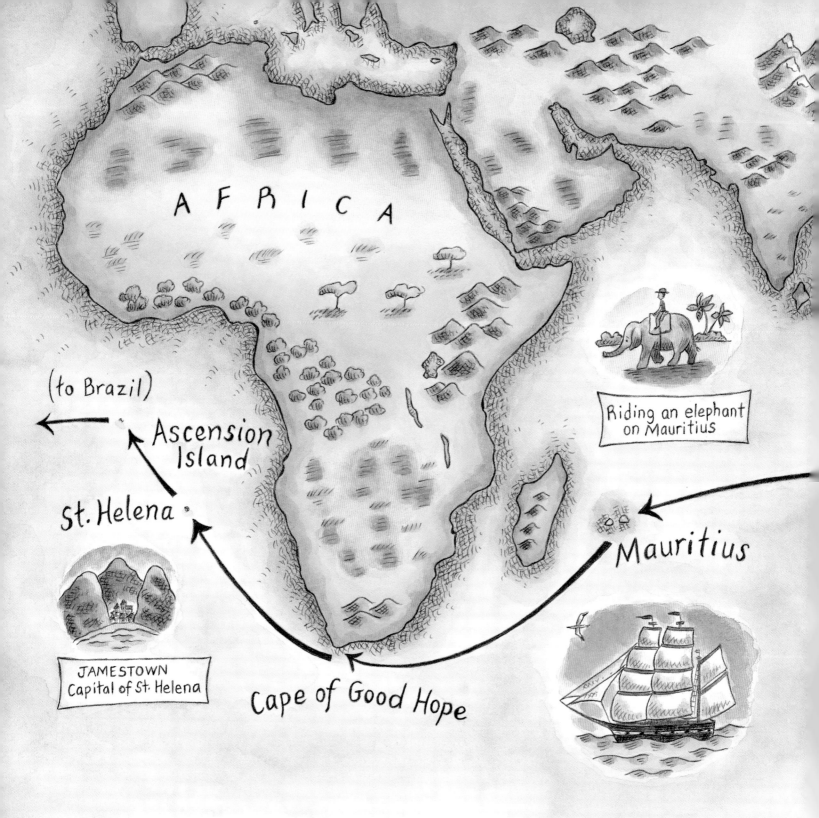

AFRICA

(to Brazil)

Ascension
Island

St. Helena

JAMESTOWN
Capital of St. Helena

Cape of Good Hope

Riding an elephant
on Mauritius

Mauritius

By now, everyone was homesick, but the ship still had a few more
stops to make.

There were coral reefs that seemed so fragile, yet were strong
enough to protect small sandy islands from pounding ocean waves.
And the coral was alive! It was made of tiny polyps that grew on top of

Keeling Islands

A S I A

AUSTRALIA

Tahiti

Sydney

King George
Sound

Hobart,
TASMANIA

New
Zealand

Birgus Coconut Crab
Keeling Islands

mountains sunken far beneath the water. Charles saw again how the
land could rise and fall. It was always changing.

After one more stop in Brazil, the *Beagle* sailed back to England
five years from the time she had left, fair winds blowing her
homeward.

When Charles returned to his family, his father said that the shape of
his head had changed. Perhaps it had grown larger, with knowledge!
Charles knew he had much more work to do in the coming years.
There were still so many questions to answer, and he needed to be sure

of his ideas. His journey of discovery would continue for the rest of his life. He would study worms and pigeons and barnacles, and write about what he learned.

And what he wrote would change the world forever.

Notes

Charles Darwin was only twenty-two years old when he set out on the HMS *Beagle* for the five-year voyage that lasted from 1831 to 1836. It would change his life. Imagine how amazing the world must have seemed to a young person who lived in a time before the Internet and television, and who had only ever read about exotic places.

Though Charles is best known today for what he learned in the Galápagos Islands, most of his time was spent traveling on land in South America. What he learned there served just as much to inform his ideas about evolution.

Charles didn't realize how famous he had become while he was away. John Stevens Henslow, his professor of botany from Cambridge University and friend, had been sharing the letters and specimens Charles sent home to England with other natural scientists. They were impressed with his discoveries.

It would take another twenty-three years after his return for Charles to publish his most famous book, *The Origin of Species*.

During that time, Charles married his cousin Emma Wedgwood, had ten children, and struggled on and off with mysterious illnesses. (Possibly caused by the bite of a benchuca bug from his time in the Andes.) He also spent years organizing his notes and specimens from the voyage and writing about worms, glaciers, coral reefs, and pigeons, among many other subjects. He kept notebooks for all of his ideas. Charles knew that his theories about transmutation (or evolution, as we know it today) would upset people who believed that the earth and its creatures were formed all at once, so he wanted to be absolutely sure of his work.

In science, a *theory* is something that has been proven through observation and experiment, while remaining open to the chance that new discoveries may change those findings. Throughout his life, Charles was always curious and open-minded about new possibilities.

He wasn't the only person working on ideas about evolution. The early 1800s were a time of intense interest in natural history, and many people were studying and writing about life on Earth. One such man was Alfred Russel Wallace. He had some of the same ideas as Charles. But when *The Origin of Species* was finally published in 1859, there were no bad feelings between the men. In fact, Charles thought it would make the case for evolution even stronger to have more scientists publish their findings. The central idea in Charles's book was that all living creatures change and adapt over time in order to survive. It was a completely new way of looking at life on Earth! The *Beagle*'s voyage had laid the groundwork for his ideas.

Charles's childhood fascination with the natural world continued through his adulthood. He was passionate about his interests, and worked diligently until the day he died. He didn't care as much about fame as he did about contributing to the world of science. He was surprised by how much attention his theories received.

Maps tell stories and spark the imagination! So much of Charles's story has to do with the geography of the places he visited. His story came to life for me while reading his own words about the trip in his book *The Voyage of the Beagle*. In spite of the many dangers he encountered—bad weather, occasional lack of food and water, accidents, disease, and political uprisings—he felt more of a sense of adventure than danger. His never-ending sense of curiosity and good-naturedness had me hooked. I hope to make Charles's world come alive through this book.

Note: The map of the Galápagos Islands on pages 32–33 is labeled as it would have been in Charles's time. All other place names are consistent with the *Merriam-Webster* dictionary.

Sources

Browne, Janet. *Voyaging*. Vol. 1 of *Charles Darwin: A Biography*. Princeton: Princeton University Press, 1996.

Darwin, Charles. *The Voyage of the Beagle: Journal of Researches into the Natural History and Geology of the Countries Visited During the Voyage of H.M.S. Beagle Round the World*. New York: Modern Library, 2001.

Darwin, Charles. *The Autobiography of Charles Darwin: 1809–1882*. Edited by Nora Barlow. New York: W. W. Norton & Company, Inc., 1993.

Darwin Correspondence Project. University of Cambridge, 2015. http://www.darwinproject.ac.uk.

Moorehead, Alan. *Darwin and the Beagle*. New York: Penguin Books, 1978.

Wyhe, John van, ed. 2002. The Complete Work of Charles Darwin Online. Last modified August 24, 2015. http://darwin-online.org.uk.

Further Reading

Chin, Jason. *Island: A Story of the Galápagos*. New York: Roaring Brook Press, 2012.

Heiligman, Deborah. *Charles and Emma: The Darwins' Leap of Faith*. New York: Henry Holt and Company, 2009.

Lasky, Kathryn. *One Beetle Too Many: The Extraordinary Adventures of Charles Darwin*. Illustrated by Matthew Trueman. Somerville: Candlewick Press, 2009.

Sís, Peter. *The Tree of Life: A Book Depicting the Life of Charles Darwin—Naturalist, Geologist & Thinker*. New York: Farrar, Straus & Giroux, 2003.

Fun Facts

Charles was inspired to pursue the study of natural history by his favorite botany and geology professors, John Stevens Henslow and Adam Sedgwick.

A naturalist is a person who studies the plants, animals, and land of the earth. Today, *naturalist* and *biologist* are often used interchangeably, but in Charles's time, the field of biology did not yet exist.

The *Beagle* was only ninety feet long, but it held seventy-four people. Charles had to remove a drawer to fit his feet when he slept because his cabin was so small.

Three passengers on board were being returned to their home in Tierra del Fuego. Their names were York Minster, Jemmy Button, and Fuegia Basket.

The *Beagle* had a library of almost four hundred books—about geology, travel, history, maps, and science. They were written in English, French, Spanish, German, Latin, and Greek.

The *Beagle* navigated with the help of twenty-two nautical chronometers. These were special clocks designed to find the longitude (east–west measurement) of a location.

The *Beagle* was not allowed to land at its first stop at Tenerife, due to fear of a disease called cholera. Charles was disappointed. He had read about the island when he was a boy.

Sometimes Charles and Captain FitzRoy argued. Charles was disgusted by the brutal treatment of slaves in Brazil, while FitzRoy thought slavery was acceptable.

In the Cape Verde Islands, an octopus squirted Charles with ink, and a cuttlefish changed colors. This is how they protect themselves from predators.

As the *Beagle* sailed away from Río de la Plata, it was surrounded by so many butterflies that the sailors said it was "snowing butterflies."

In South America, Charles saw birds that used wings for reasons other than flying. Penguins and ducks use them like fins to dive through water, and ostriches, like sails to balance while running.

In Patagonia, female rheas laid eggs in shallow holes, while the males sat on them until they hatched, then cared for the young chicks.

Charles saw a fish in Brazil—called *Diodon antennatus* (known as the porcupine fish)—that puffed itself full of water to look bigger, for protection.

Charles traveled to the Andes with two guides, ten sure-footed mules, and one *madrina*—a mule with a bell around her neck to keep the others calm through the steep mountain passes.

In the Andes, water boiled but potatoes wouldn't cook overnight, because of low atmospheric pressure and little oxygen in the air. Thankfully, fleas couldn't survive the altitude, either.

Charles observed that plants and animals were different on each side of the Andes Mountains. They had each adapted to their different environments.

Charles noticed that on the Keeling Islands, trees grew from seeds that had washed ashore from thousands of miles away. The seeds had to be sturdy enough to survive the trip.

Charles saw how human activity affected the environments of Mauritius and Saint Helena, due to rats and goats brought by visiting ships.

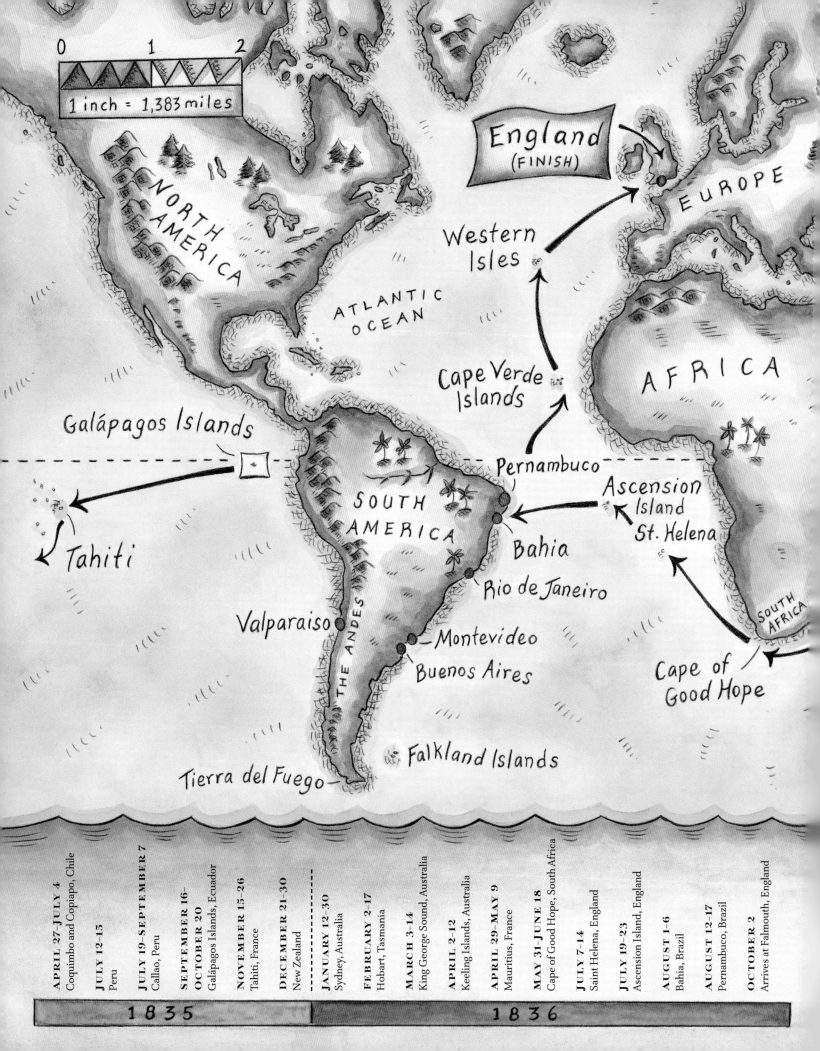

0   1   2

1 inch = 1,383 miles

England
(FINISH)

EUROPE

NORTH
AMERICA

Western
Isles

Cape Verde
Islands

ATLANTIC
OCEAN

AFRICA

Galápagos Islands

Pernambuco

SOUTH
AMERICA

Bahia

Ascension
Island
St. Helena

Tahiti

Rio de Janeiro

Valparaiso

Montevideo

SOUTH
AFRICA

THE ANDES

Buenos Aires

Cape of
Good Hope

Falkland Islands

Tierra del Fuego

APRIL 27–JULY 4
Coquimbo and Copiapo, Chile

JULY 12–15
Peru

JULY 19–SEPTEMBER 7
Callao, Peru

**SEPTEMBER 16–
OCTOBER 20**
Galápagos Islands, Ecuador

NOVEMBER 15–26
Tahiti, France

DECEMBER 21–30
New Zealand

JANUARY 12–30
Sydney, Australia

FEBRUARY 2–17
Hobart, Tasmania

MARCH 3–14
King George Sound, Australia

APRIL 2–12
Keeling Islands, Australia

APRIL 29–MAY 9
Mauritius, France

MAY 31–JUNE 18
Cape of Good Hope, South Africa

JULY 7–14
Saint Helena, England

JULY 19–23
Ascension Island, England

AUGUST 1–6
Bahia, Brazil

AUGUST 12–17
Pernambuco, Brazil

OCTOBER 2
Arrives at Falmouth, England

1835   **1836**